PEARLS
Short Stories for
Personal Management

Sunil Thomas, Ph.D.

SUNIPRINT
A Division of Abraham Thomas Foundation

PEARLS
Short Stories for Personal Management

Copyright © Sunil Thomas/SUNIPRINT
2023

All rights reserved. This publication may not be reproduced, distributed or transmitted in any from or by any means including photocopying, recording, or other electronic or mechanical methods without the prior written permission of the publisher.

Cover Design: Sunil Thomas

ISBN: 979-8-9866300-1-4

SUNIPRINT
A Division of Abraham Thomas Foundation
11 Cambridge Road, Broomall, PA-19008, USA
E-mail: suniprintbooks@gmail.com

CONTENTS

PREFACE 3
1. THE PEARL NECKLACE 5
2. CLIMBING THE MOUNTAIN 7
3. THE DANCE OF THE SHADOWS 9
4. WHY I AM NOT PAID THE SAME AS MY COLLEAGUE 12
5. THE NEW BORN CALF 15
6. THE BOARDROOM TABLE 17
7. LIFE IN A BOTTLE 19
8. WOW FACTOR 21
9. THE TOOTHPASTE 22
10. THE RUBBER TAPPER 23
11. THE TOY TRAIN 26
12. THE BULLOCK CART 28
13. SEEING TALENTS IN YOUR OPPONENT 30
14. ASSESSING THE LEADER 32
15. THE EGG 34
16. CHRISTMAS TREE 35
17. THE VAGABOND BUSINESSMAN 36
18. THE TOMATO 38
19. THE ROLLS-ROYCE 39
20. THE CLOCK 41
21. THE HIGHWAY 43
22. VALUES 45
23. STUDY, STUDY, STUDY 47
24. BE CAUTIOUS FOLLOWING THE VOICE OF THE CROWD 49
25. THE IMAGE 51
26. MAN'S LIFE 52
27. THE APPLE TREE 53

28. THE CRASH 54
29. WINDOW OF OPPORTUNITY 56
30. THE WORLD DOES NOT WAIT FOR ANYONE 58
31. GOAL 59
32. CORNERED AT THE CORNER 60
33. ORGANIZATION AS A TREE.................. 63
34. THE NUTMEG.. 64
35. THE SEA WALL 65
36. WORK IN PROGRESS 67
37. COFFEE TIME 69
38. THE DRIVER... 70
39. THE CARROT 71
40. THE ROCKET 73
41. THE SUN WILL EMERGE FROM THE CLOUD 75
42. FREE LUNCH 77
43. EPICENTER OF LEARNING 78
44. LAYERS... 80
45. THE COLLEGE KID................................... 81
46. VERY IMPORTANT PERSON 83
47. THE WOOD 85
48. INFLUENCE.. 87
49. EXERCISE 89
50. JOSEPH THE GOVERNOR..................... 90
51. THE FIRST CHRISTMAS 92

PREFACE

Early experiences and interactions heavily influence the development of an individual's principles, values, and beliefs. As people grow and gain exposure to new environments, such as college or the workplace, they often encounter diverse perspectives that can challenge or complement their existing beliefs. This exposure can lead to personal philosophies evolving or even changing entirely.

As social beings, we have countless interactions with others throughout our lives. Whether it's within a family, organization, or country, our behavior and personal philosophies can have a profound impact on the people around us. In professional settings, especially when working with diverse cultures and values, it is crucial to foster an environment of motivation, inspiration, and encouragement.

Most organizations run by professionals fold up within seventy five years. Advances in medical technologies have increased lifespan of people. You have to be strong physically, mentally and spiritually till the end of your time. You have to educate yourself, build, prosper, and train others. Personal management involves setting and achieving both short-term and long-term goals while applying management principles to enhance productivity and success.

The process of personal management requires discipline, planning, and self-awareness. By setting clear and achievable goals, creating a roadmap to reach them, managing your time efficiently, staying focused, and continuously learning and adapting, you can make significant progress in various areas of your life. Additionally, personal management is not just about achieving external success but also about maintaining a healthy work-life balance, nurturing relationships, managing stress, and enhancing emotional intelligence to lead a fulfilling and meaningful life. It empowers individuals to take control of their lives, make informed decisions, and proactively work towards their aspirations.

Personal management is a dynamic and ongoing process that empowers individuals to lead purposeful lives by effectively utilizing resources, setting and achieving goals, and enhancing overall well-being and success.

This book, "Pearls: Short Stories for Personal Management," is a quick read book for anyone interested in personal management. Concepts on personal management are told as short stories in this book. The short stories are written to encourage and motivate the reader to improve character, skills and capabilities.

1. THE PEARL NECKLACE

Denny was the senior executive of the research and development department of a company. He was a people person. He loved interacting with people. There were many super talented scientists in the company. Unfortunately, most of them were self-centered. The scientists were like islands not connected by any bridges.

Denny knew that if the company had to be successful they had to launch new products for the masses. He also knew that new products could only be launched by strong collaboration with several scientists across disciplines. Denny reached out to scientists in the company. The result could be seen on the annual report and the stock price of the company.

Decades later, Denny retired and moved to a far-away city with his son. The company did not perform well. Eventually, it was merged with a competitor.

In every organization there are talented and super talented people. They are like pearls. However if the expensive pearls have to be made into a necklace, it has to be connected by a "not-so expensive" silk thread. Most often, the job of a silk-thread is taken by a humble "people person" sitting in a corner office, and that person is the invisible core of the organization. In the absence of a coordinator, the CEO of the organization has to take up the role.

2. CLIMBING THE MOUNTAIN

A group of fifty college students were taken to remote villages and mountains for a field trip. The professor accompanied the students so that he could explain the flora, fauna, geology as well as the history of the region.

On the second day, the student group reached the base of a tall mountain. The professor put forward a challenge to the students. "Whoever could climb up the peak of the mountain and come back will be rewarded."

All the students gazed at the mountain. They said, "It would take at least one hour to reach the peak. The terrain is also difficult." Thirty students dropped the idea immediately. Twenty students said, "We will take up the challenge."

The shortest student of the class, Stanley also rose to the challenge. Everyone in the group was amused when Stanley took up the challenge of climbing the mountain. They said, "Stanley, you have to climb up the peak, not come back in five minutes."

Those students who took up the challenge took food and water for the journey.

Ten minutes later several students returned. Within forty-five minutes most of the students returned without accomplishing the challenge, except one, Stanley!

The students stated that the mountain was too high, and they were fatigued after some time.

Even when Stanley's classmates gave up, Stanley pursued. He kept on climbing until he reached the peak in one hour. Upon reaching the peak of the mountain he waved to the crowd below. It was a majestic view up from the peak of the mountain. Stanley took pictures of the valley below. After fifteen minutes at the peak, he returned back to the base.

The professor asked Stanley how he accomplished the feat when everyone else gave up. Stanley stated, "I did not look up the mountain while climbing. I just saw the terrain immediately in front of me. If I looked up the mountain and scaled it, I would have given up."

Sometimes the work staring at us looks impossible to complete when viewed from a distance. Just do it; one part at a time.

3. THE DANCE OF THE SHADOWS

Simon was a young accountant at a large firm. He worked hard; his colleagues liked him as he was very helpful to them by taking up any extra assignments. Simon was resource conscious and used to give ideas on running the firm in a small budget; he also gave ideas on how to increase revenue. Some of the ideas were novel and the managers ignored Simon's ideas.

During weekends, Simon visited motor, aviation and boat shows as he was very enthusiastic about vehicles since his childhood. A couple of years into the job, the firm made a huge loss and the management decided to shed scores of jobs. Unfortunately, Simon's job was also on the chopping block. Simon's supervisor, Sophie wanted to help her friends at the department, hence she suggested Simon's name to the HR to be terminated.

Simon was sad and frustrated that he lost his job even though he worked diligently and made huge revenues for the firm. He felt ashamed and walked with his head down. He walked aimlessly for several days thinking about his bad fate and also about his former supervisor who threw him under the bus.

One day, while sitting on the park bench Simon saw a bird land on a straight thin branch of a nearby tree. The branch bent slightly while the bird sat on it. The bird flew after sometime, and the tree branch straightened-up. The bird again came back and sat on the same tree branch and again the branch bent slightly due to the weight of the bird.

Simon understood that he was allowing the shadows of the people in his past job dance on his head that in turn blocked his progress. Simon became aware that the depth of failure would increase if he would let his opponent play in his mind. Simon also realized that if he installed his opponent's idol deep in his mind and spend more time thinking about the person, failure would penetrate deep inside him impacting his health.

Simon bid adieu to his negative thoughts. Simon got up from the park bench and headed to the inner city thinking about his future.

While walking in front of a hotel Simon saw a group of tourists waiting for their van. Simon overheard that the van that was supposed to pick up did not turn up at the scheduled time. Simon had an idea; he went inside the hotel and inquired if the hotel would like to have a prompt transportation service for their guests. The manager stated that he would be happy if someone would offer good transportation service for his guests.

Simon immediately contacted several tourist transportation services and struck a deal. He would get a percentage for filling up the vans. Months later, Simon leased a couple of vans and launched his own transportation service.

Several years later, Simon diversified into freight services. He launched his own truck service; that was very successful. Eventually, he took over a bankrupt shipping firm when a good offer came up. When Simon felt the need for quick global transportation, he ventured into air-freight. He recently placed orders for five wide body freighters.

Simon still has the tourist van service. He uses that business to train his new recruits.

4. WHY I AM NOT PAID THE SAME AS MY COLLEAGUE

This is a story from the nineteenth century. I am not sure if it is true. The story goes like this....One day a guard employed in the Kingdom of Travancore, in the southern tip of the Indian subcontinent came to see the King.

The King asked, "What can I do for you?"

The guard replied, "I work for 12-15 hours, six days a week. My salary is too less. The minister of this Kingdom is paid one hundred times my salary, even though he put in fewer hours."

The King thought for a while. He said to the guard, "That is unfortunate."

The King saw a bullock cart (ox cart) moving slowly at a distance. The King asked the guard to find where the bullock cart was headed. The guard ran to the bullock cart and asked the owner where he was headed.

The bullock cart's owner replied, "To the market."

The guard ran to the King and stated that the bullock cart was headed to the market.

The King asked the guard what was in the bullock cart. The guard said, I don't know. I will ask."

The guard ran to the bullock cart and came back and said, "It has vegetables and rice."

The King asked what vegetables were in the bullock cart. The guard stated, "I don't know. I will inquire."

The guard again ran to the bullock cart and came back and said, "The bullock cart has yams, lettuce, chilly, snake gourd, cucumber and green banana."

The King asked the quantity of rice in the bullock cart. The guard said, "Sorry, I don't know."

The guard again ran, inquired and came back. He stated to the King, "Highness, the bullock cart has two sacks, each containing 40 kilograms of rice."

While the King and guard was speaking, the minister passed by. The King called the minister and pointed down the road. "Do you see a bullock cart down the road, ask where it is headed."

The minister stated humbly, "Sure I will."

The minister came back after some time. The King asked the minister again where the bullock cart was going.

The minister replied, "The bullock cart is headed to the market. The bullock cart is 5 years old. It has produce in it. The produce includes yams, lettuce, chilly, snake gourd, cucumber and green banana. In addition there are two sacks of rice, 40 Kg each. The worth of the goods at current market price is Rs. 10. The owner will buy clothes for his family upon return from the market and he will be back after two days."

The King turned to the guard and stated. "Now you know why the minister is paid more than you."

5. THE NEW BORN CALF

When a calf of an herbivore is born in the wild, it has to stand on all fours and walk within half-an hour of its birth. The animal and its family are at risk if it stays for a longer period of time on the same spot. The blood and other fluids attract the predators and the calf will be lunch within a matter of time. Hence, the calf has to walk as soon as possible away from the birth place along with its extended family.

When you take the mantle of a new organization, there are umpteen eyes watching you from within and outside the organization. Very few people would like you to succeed. You have to run the organization better than the predecessor.

When you are an outsider of an organization given a leadership position, you will have to understand the culture of the organization as well as behavior of the people in your new organization. You will have no idea of the politics and tussle in the organization. You have to use your instincts to find the people you can trust. Do not be carried away by groups that have vested interests within an organization. Stay neutral and understand the situation. Form a core team and listen to them. Mold a consensus and take effective decisions. Make it clear why you took the decision before executing it. Make sure to move around and meet everyone at all levels of the organization early on so as to gain their respect. Get feedback from everyone. Show that you are receptive to new ideas.

You will be evaluated based on what you accomplished in the first one hundred days. If the organization was at a loss, you will have to make quick changes and steer the organization to a new direction.

6. THE BOARDROOM TABLE

Bob and Doris wished to have a large boardroom table in their office. They planned to have a table with the best tree growth ring pattern. They found a large black walnut wood with good grain pattern at a lumber depot. Bob and Doris purchased the wood and made a fine boardroom table, the dark grains of the table were always a topic of conversation before every meeting.

The tree rings (growth rings) can be counted to determine the age of the tree. The light-colored rings denote the good weather conditions with abundant rain, whereas the dark colored rings denote the poor weather condition with less rain. The dense dark colored rings provide strength to the tree. Every tree is unique; they have their own grain pattern. The grain pattern determines the price of the furniture.

It is said that success should not get to our head and failure should not get to our heart. Every human has success and failures in life. We are the product of failures and success. Success should make us humble, and failure should motivate us to move forward.

Success could ignite the ego within us. Success also could make us think superior to others; sometimes going to the extent of abusing others. Everyone wishes to be successful in front of the society. Success is not constant; people sometimes go to the extreme not to fail. You only get to see pseudo-faces when you are a success.

We learn from our failures. In fact, the failures determine our identity. The failure in our life makes us stronger, bolder, confident and courageous. We get more creative from failures. Failure gives us experience. Failure helps us innovate and be more resourceful. When you fail, you don't have to please others. Failure also helps us understand our true relatives and friends. When you have reached the nadir, the only space available is to move up.

7. LIFE IN A BOTTLE

A long-necked bottle can be considered as an analogy of our life. Our initial life and actions have limits when our life is in the bottle.

At one point in our life, we may be squeezed, as if moving through the bottle neck. We may feel stressed due to economic situations, relations, death or problems in the family, disease, loss of job, work-place situations, wars, famine, repeated failure, court verdicts, etc. We fail or succeed depending on how we respond to the circumstances in the bottle neck.

"If God takes you to it, he will take you through it."

Big ships are directed by small tugboats at the port. When your life is in the bottle neck, do not try to handle it alone; chances are that you will make wrong decisions. It is better to hand over your life to the Creator, and he will run your life smoothly.

Many "smart people" have failed due to the wrong decisions taken when they were in the bottle neck phase of their lives. Wrong decisions taken in the bottle neck phase could also pull one back inside the bottle thereby stunting growth. The long bottle neck is littered with skeletons; millions of people have lost their lives due to the wrong moves during difficult situations.

Once you pass the bottle neck, you are in a world where life has no boundaries. You will be the respected leader of the domain. People will idolize you based on how you handled difficult situations.

8. WOW FACTOR

It was fall season. Mr. Richard took the children to see the beautiful fall season scenery of New England.

When Richard's family reached New England, it was cloudy. The children had no response upon seeing the beautiful fall colors.

Half an hour later, the clouds cleared, and it was sunny. The children enjoyed and marveled at the brightly colored trees and the mountains. Mr. Richard took the children under a maple tree. He asked the children to look up. 'Wow, the leaves look like thousands of brightly lit lanterns," exclaimed the children.

Even though one is talented or super talented, people don't appreciate you. However, upon completion of an important project or assignment that very few can execute, you become a star.

9. THE TOOTHPASTE

Our career is akin to a tube of toothpaste. You don't throw the half empty tube of toothpaste. Similarly, you don't sit idle and waste your talent after a termination or layoff. The world needs your talents. Your past experiences and vision is enough to build something beautiful.

Go ahead and build marvelous enterprises.

10. THE RUBBER TAPPER

Mr. and Mrs. Wilson retired to the village after the busy life in the city. They inherited a small property from their parents. Mr. Wilson planted rubber trees just before retirement. The rubber trees were ready for tapping once the Wilson's moved in. The latex is harvested by cutting a small groove on the bark of the tree. The latex is collected in a plastic bowl and converted to rubber sheet or stored as liquid latex in drums.

There was a shortage of rubber tappers in the village. Mr. Wilson hired Mr. Teddy as the rubber tapper. Many people warned Mr. Wilson not to hire Mr. Teddy due to his past behavior. As there was no choice, Mr. Wilson hired Teddy. The rubber tress planted by Mr. Wilson was a high yielding variety. Mr. Teddy was selfish and self-centered; he never wished others to progress.

Mr. Teddy would cut the rubber tree bark so that only a limited quantity of latex would be collected. After paying the salary of Mr. Teddy, Mr. Wilson had hardly any money left for his family. Fortunately, Mr. Wilson's children helped him run the small farm.

Mr. Wilson was sad that his farm was not very successful. He sent Mr. Teddy to rubber plantation meetings so as to improve his skills. Mr. Teddy would participate in the meetings for a couple of hours, skip the classes and shop around town.

After several years, Mr. Teddy got a job opportunity at a large farm. He quit from Mr. Wilson's farm. Fortunately, Mr. Wilson found a young rubber tapper, Mr. Carl. Mr. Carl was very diligent; he did a splendid job of tapping the rubber trees. He would show the production chart every month and recommend the fertilizers to improve production. The rubber production at Mr. Wilson's farm increased many fold.

People run their life based on their personal philosophies and values. They have already decided what to do or what not to do before being offered an opportunity. Some people go to the extreme of pushing their organization to the "next phase". There are also people who do the "minimum work" when they are hired in an organization. Though they are talented they don't grow the organization. They work "just enough" that the organization makes minimum profit. With no innovation, the organization gets stunted. They fold up after some time.

At universities, the professors should enlighten and motivate the students. At some universities the professors hardly engage the students. They often request the adjuncts or senior graduate and postdoctoral students to teach junior classes. Such universities also have few research projects. Research projects could lead to discoveries and start-ups. Lack of genuine research projects dampens the purpose of universities. Eventually the students leave the field and move to other sectors.

Similar is the situation with some developing countries where the leaders and their associates accumulate wealth, whereas the people suffer due to unemployment and hunger. These selfish administrators set up policies such that a large population fails. Patriotism ends when hunger sets in. People immigrate to distant lands when selfish administrators take charge of the country. The selfish leaders proclaim that they will eliminate corruption, hunger and unemployment though they are the cause of the malady. The country withers when corrupt leaders are in charge.

Determined and committed people make the world a better place to live.

11. THE TOY TRAIN

When Brad was a young boy he saw an advertisement of a toy train in a comic book. He longed to have the toy train. Brad begged his mother and father for the toy train. However, his parents could not afford to buy the expensive train at that age; they had other priorities.

Years passed, Brad completed his education. He got a good position at a big company. A couple of months later, Brad planned to go home to see his parents and nephews. He thought of buying toys for his nephews and visited a toy shop.

Brad was surprised to see the toy train he wished to have years back in the toy shop. Brad's wallet had money to buy all the trains in the toy shop. Alas! Brad was too old to play with a toy train. Nevertheless, he bought two trains for his nephews.

People are passionate about the arts or hobbies. However, many of them lament that though they are interested in painting, tour national parks, climb Mount Everest, drive the length of the country, write a book, interested in snorkeling, indulge in culinary arts, run a marathon, etc., they keep their hobbies in the backburner due to their career and will be pursuing their hobbies only after retirement.

For them, career is the only priority until retirement.

Once people retire, it is not sure whether they will pursue their hobbies. Many of them will be in poor health, some die, some give up their hobbies. If people are interested in adventure or hobbies they should pursue it right away and not wait until retirement. In fact, hobbies and career have a yin yang effect, they complement each other. Pursuing a hobby along with your career improves your career.

12. THE BULLOCK CART

Master Santhosh used to love to go to town during the holidays. He used to nag his neighbor Mr. Ram to take him to town. Ram was always sympathetic to Master Santhosh and would take him to town on his bullock cart. Mr. Ram would provide him delicious mangoes while travelling and would also buy food when he reached town. Those days there were no cars in the village. However, Santhosh could not take his eyes off the cars in town. He longed to buy one when he grew up.

Years passed, Santhosh completed his junior college and wished to go to college in the city. One day Mr. Ram asked Santhosh whether he wished to go to town as he was going to that direction.

Santhosh remarked, "I do not wish to ride on your old bullock cart anymore. I will travel to town with my neighbor, Mr. Rakesh. He just bought a brand new Fiat."

Mr. Ram was sad hearing the comment of Mr. Santhosh. But unknown to Mr. Santhosh was that Mr. Ram was headed to town to see his son, who had a fleet of trucks. Mr. Ram wanted to introduce Mr. Santhosh to his son.

Mr. Ram collected the produce from his field and headed to town on his bullock cart. On the way Mr. Ram saw Santhosh and Rakesh zip by on a brand new Fiat. The car was over speeding and lost control over a small bridge and fell into the river below. The car was struck in the river mud.

Fifteen minutes later, from the sunken car, Mr. Santhosh saw Mr. Ram pass by the bridge on his old bullock cart.

13. SEEING TALENTS IN YOUR OPPONENT

August 10, 1741: The battle of Colachel was fought between the Maharaja of Venad, Marthanda Varma and Dutch East India Company (Vereenigde Oost-Indische Compagnie, VOC) in the southern tip of India. The Maharaja, his army and subjects defeated the small army of Dutch East India Company. The soldiers of Dutch East India Company were taken hostage and imprisoned by the Maharaja.

The Kingdom of Venad was a small state in the southern tip of India. The Maharaja knew that he was lucky to win the battle; his fortune would have been hit if the opponent's army was superior. He knew the weakness of his army. He didn't rejoice in his success. He understood the superiority of the European forces.

The Maharaja asked the imprisoned Dutch officer Eustachius Benedictus de Lannoy to modernize the Venad army. Captain de Lannoy was a military strategist, he not only modernized the army, he conquered the northern territories aided by the Prime Minister (Dalawa) Ramayyan, ultimately creating the Kingdom of Travancore.

Captain de Lannoy constructed a defense fortification (Nedumkotta or Travancore Lines) in the neighboring northern Kingdom of Cochin so as to protect Travancore from enemies. The fortification indeed protected Travancore 35 years later during the Mysore invasion.

Technologies and management strategies become redundant. New technologies and strategies have to be mastered to run an organization stay relevant. Often times if your organization has poor strategies you will have to learn from your opponent's organization.

Companies sometimes recruit people from the competitor's organization to grow their organization. Another strategy is to collaborate on projects with the competing companies including start ups.

14. ASSESSING THE LEADER

Jonathan was driving during the weekend. There were not many vehicles on the road. He came at an intersection; the signal light was red. The car in front of him turned right since it was allowed to turn right if there were no vehicles passing by.

Jonathan thought that since it was a weekend there would be no traffic on the road and just followed the car in front of him.

Bad luck! A van slammed on to Jonathan's car. Since Jonathan wore a seat belt, he was unhurt.

The driver in front of Jonathan saw a van coming from the distance. The driver knew he had time to turn right and hence turned to that direction. However, Jonathan never bothered to notice the traffic coming from the left; if he had calculated the speed of the traffic flow, he would have stopped his car. Jonathan blindly followed the car in front of him and that decision turned to be fatal.

One should not follow any leader blindly. Be it the leader of a company, non-profit, politics, or spiritual organization, you have to assess the leaders intentions and behavior periodically. Every one has hidden agendas and the agendas change with time. You have every right to correct your leader if they are on the wrong path. Your voice should be audible to the leader.

15. THE EGG

Mrs. Betsy had some guests for breakfast. She decided to cook different types of egg dishes for breakfast as the guests liked eggs. Mrs. Betsy decided to cook scrambled eggs, omelette, boiled eggs, and Kerala roast eggs. Mrs. Betsy boiled the eggs and placed it on the kitchen counter to cool. She also placed some raw eggs beside the boiled eggs.

While handling a hot pan, Mrs. Betsy inadvertently struck the eggs and all of them fell on the kitchen floor. All the raw eggs were smashed; whereas the boiled eggs had just cracks on the shell.

Mrs. Betsy washed the boiled eggs, removed the shell and used it in her dishes. The raw eggs that fell on the floor were of no use. Mrs. Betsy had to clean the floor with soap and water to remove the egg stain.

When you have strong philosophy and spiritual values, even if you fall, you will get up and walk. Having philosophical and spiritual values, doesn't mean that you will not fall. The fall will not hurt you; you will rise up after each fall.

16. CHRISTMAS TREE

Every December, people buy Christmas trees and adorn it with lights and ornaments. Around Christmas time, or during Christmas, visitors come to the house, have pictures taken in front of the tree. The visitors praise the Christmas tree and the lighting and ornaments. One week after the New Year, the Christmas tree, without ornaments and lighting would be lying on the curb waiting for the garbage truck to be picked up.

The same is true with people holding offices. When they are in the office, people visit them and praise them and may also get benefits for the praise. The media may be behind them to hear their thoughts. Once out of office, people just ignore them. Even the relatives seldom visit them.

17. THE VAGABOND BUSINESSMAN

One day, sometime during the last years of the twentieth century, I headed to the bus stop in front of a medical research institute in New Delhi, India, after a busy day in the laboratory. While waiting for the bus, I saw a young man walking to the bus stop, carrying a plastic sack on his head. The street in front to the bus stop was not very clean. There were many broken wooden boxes, newspaper, etc., lying around.

The young man took a broken wooden box as well as some newspapers lying on the street. He came and stood by the side of the bus shelter. He placed the sack on the ground and opened it. It contained a rusted iron pan with charcoal and below it a bundle of corn.

The seller lighted the newspaper and placed it on the charcoal. Once it started burning slowly, he placed his corn and grilled it. He then placed the corn on the broken wooden box.

People who passed by or was in the bus stop bought corn from the corn seller. The corn seller squeezed some lemon and sprinkled pepper powder over the corn before selling to his customers.

The corn seller did not do any market research, or have anything to start a business while venturing out of his home. All he had may have been a rusted iron pan, optimism and determination. He may have purchased the corn and charcoal from the market after his day job.

You have to be street smart to grow yourself and your organization.

18. THE TOMATO

Ryan decided to plant tomatoes in his garden. He planted some during early spring and another batch during mid-summer.

The tomato plants bloomed in a month and Ryan collected ripe tomatoes from the spring planted ones after a couple of months.

The tomatoes planted during mid-summer also bore fruits. However, once the temperature dipped in early autumn the fruits did not ripen. They also cracked due to changes in temperature; they were of no use to Ryan.

It is better to work hard and complete your studies early in life. Similarly, if you are an employee or in business, complete your projects quickly. You do not know the hurdles you will be facing if you postpone the tasks.

19. THE ROLLS-ROYCE

Ray and Scott were friends at a boarding school. When they were in the middle-school, their teacher handed them a book on expensive cars. Ray and Scott decided to read it during the weekend. They read about Rolls-Royce cars, its history and how they built it. Most people buy high-end cars based on their dreams at a young age. Ray and Scott also were inspired by Rolls-Royce cars.

Ray commented, "One day..." Suddenly Scott intervened, "I will buy a Rolls-Royce."

Years passed. Scott became a successful salesman. His company made huge profits. Scott didn't forget his dream of buying a Rolls-Royce. He bought the latest Rolls-Royce and showed his friends and relatives. Everyone was happy for Scott. Scott attracted many new friends. He married one of his best friends.

Several years later, Scott's fortune declined. He had to sell his expensive car. When the business crashed most of his friends deserted him, including his wife. Scott did several odd jobs to live.

Scott's friend Ray was not interested in having a Rolls-Royce car but loved its engineering. He liked how the car was carefully engineered. He wished to set up a factory for automobile parts.

Ray worked hard to set up a small auto parts factory. His factory manufactured the best auto parts in the country. His auto parts were expensive as he used good quality materials; Ray's products lasted longer than his competitors.

Initially, Ray struggled to get enough orders for his company. Since the competitors products did not last long, several of the auto manufacturers turned to Ray's company for auto parts. Eventually, Ray setup auto parts factories in several countries.

One day while having coffee in the city Ray met Scott serving the table. Ray asked Scott to follow him. Ray had a conversation with Scott at a neighboring restaurant. Upon hearing Scott's story, Ray immediately offered Scott a job.

Scott accepted the job, completed a diploma in foreign trade during weekends, worked hard, had a new family and grew Ray's company exponentially. Ray's company was happy to award bonus and stocks to Scott. Though Scot became richer in his second innings, he still drives an ordinary car. He also has set up a philanthropic organization for the needy.

20. THE CLOCK

The three hands of the analog clock denote seconds, minutes and hours. Some clocks have days of the month.

The second hand moves faster compared to the minute hand. The second hand has to move sixty seconds to move the minute hand. Similarly the minute hand has to move sixty minutes to move the hour hand. The hour hand moves 24 times to move the day of the month.

Every person has unique abilities and their work will influence the society positively; everyone has something to contribute. In a society no one is static; as in a clock, some people have to work hard than others. Entrepreneurs have to do several jobs to run their organization. They have to travel, read latest trends, and meet with bankers, sellers and regulators. Usually no one bothers to ask a busy person whether they had lunch or dinner. Entrepreneurs also sleep less than others due to nature of their job.

Some jobs are risky. A person working in the military, police, mining and construction face dangerous situations. However someone has to do these jobs.

A regulator or politician does not have to work hard like the common man, but they have to set policies for sustainable growth of the country. Their acts should be selfless; any abuse will tear the fabric of the society.

A successful entrepreneur or highly paid employee when donating part of the wealth for philanthropy in the form of support for education, healthcare, development of science and technology is doing a big favor to the community as it will impact not only the current generation but also the future generations.

In the analog clock model stated above, if a gear is worn, it will impact the time. Similarly, if people in a community are lethargic and selfish it is bound to affect the quality of the community and the wealth of the country.

21. THE HIGHWAY

Dalton was driving to the city with his family to see his friends. He took the highway to the city; he had to drive eight hours to reach his destination.

Dalton's family baked cakes, cookies and pastries for their friends. In addition, they carried produce from the neighborhood farm that Dalton's friends relished.

Dalton and his family started early morning. It was a pleasant journey to the city. However, after three hours the road was in bad shape. It continued for the next fifteen minutes. Dalton had to slow the car while driving the bad stretch of road. After fifteen minutes of uncomfortable driving, the condition of the road improved and everyone was comfortable. The children slept comfortably in the rear seat.

Hours later, Dalton's car slowed. The traffic ahead of Dalton stopped and Dalton wondered what was happening. After ten minutes of waiting, the traffic slowly moved. Dalton saw the traffic police directing traffic to the country road as there was a major accident on the highway.

Every passenger in the car was upset as they had to take deviation and had to drive longer to the city. However, minutes later they saw the beautiful country side with picturesque scenery. Everyone enjoyed the scenery; they stopped to take pictures. After an hour of drive they were back to the highway and reached the city one hour late than anticipated.

Our life is not perfect and smooth. Sometimes life is slow, things don't go as anticipated. Dalton did not return home when the roads were bad or when the traffic deviated; he continued his journey to the city.

Similarly, we are here on a mission. We have to figure out our mission early in our life. There may be tribulations in life, no matter what is happening around us we have to continue our mission. Sometimes our life may deviate from the normal; be optimistic, everything will be fine at the end.

22. VALUES

Emil studied at a college that had students from different strata of the society. Though Emil was not a staunch socialist, he liked the socialists as they were the voice for the voiceless, or this is what Emil always thought of them.

Several years into college, Emil was taken to a class tour. The class was taken to several industrial complexes at different cities. To lower the cost, the students had to share the room in hotels.

When it was time to checkout, Emil cleaned his bed and it looked as if no one slept on it. He saw that the other beds were messy. He asked his classmates that shared his room, who also were staunch socialists to make their bed and clean up before leaving. They replied to Emil, "We pay for this room; the workers should do this job."

Emil fell ashamed seeing the behavior of his classmates whom he held in high esteem until that moment. He waited for his classmates to leave the hotel room. Once they left, Emil cleaned the room and made sure it was tidy before closing the door.

That afternoon the students had lunch in the cafeteria of a factory. The lunch was not free;

they had to purchase their own lunch. Several of Emil's classmates did not complete their lunch and headed to the garbage can to discard the half-eaten lunch. Emil stopped his classmates wasting food. The students shot back, "It is our money, and we will do what pleases us."

Emil learned one important thing in life; most people don't walk the talk.

23. STUDY, STUDY, STUDY

Linda was the oldest daughter of her house. Linda just entered college after graduating with good grades in high school. She had a brother and sister. Linda's parents took care of their house. The neighbors were jealous of the house because it was meticulously taken care of by Linda's parents. Linda's parents always would tell their children to study well.

One day Linda's grandfather, who was in another state, got sick and was taken to the hospital. Linda's parents had to rush to take care of their father. Linda was in charge to take care of her siblings as well as the house.

When Linda's parents came back after three weeks, the house was a mess; the lawn was not mowed. There were complaints from the school teacher that their youngest children did not do the homework.

A few blocks from Linda's home was Anita's home. Anita was Linda's classmate in college. She lost her mother a couple of years back. She had to take care of three siblings. Anita's father was in sales and had to be away for a month. Anita was placed in charge of the house and the children.

When Anita's father returned after three weeks, the house was clean and tidy. The younger children scored good grades in the school tests.

Every parent is anxious about their children. They wish to see their children grow up and turn to be a success and also serve the society. They would always tell their children, "Study, study, study….", at least up to a certain age. It is a shame to ask the grown up adults to study. The children should figure out their life mission by 18 years of age.

Both Linda and Anita were always asked to study. The parents knew that they would retire one day or will be incapable to work due to health conditions. Most parents do not tell the children to study after graduating from high school. The children should be self-motivated. They should know the purpose in life. Linda, though bright in her studies, did not pursue higher education, and settled for a county clerk. Anita turned to be a pediatrician, she also volunteered for Red Cross and UNICEF.

24. BE CAUTIOUS FOLLOWING THE VOICE OF THE CROWD

In front of a temple was a large pond. Millions of pilgrims visited the temple. Once the authorities determined that the temple pond had to be cleaned. The temple pond had not been cleaned over a hundred years. The news of the cleaning of the pond was the talk of the city.

People began to speculate that the temple pond contained treasures. They also speculated that the temple pond might contain fish worth a fortune.

The temple authorities determined to go for closed tenders for cleaning the pond as well as to catch and sell fish. The authorities also stated that if treasures were found the lowest bidder for cleaning the pond could get one-tenth of the value of the treasure. As for the fish, the highest bidder could get the contract.

Hundreds of people and local companies submitted the tenders. The newspapers speculated that whoever wins the tenders would be millionaires.

Finally the tenders were opened and the winner determined. Everyone was curious to see the pond being cleaned. Newspaper and television crews were on the outer banks of the pond. Scores of pumps were used to remove water. Within a week the water was removed. The bidder could not find any treasure. All they found was hundreds of kilos of wooden beads that the pilgrims threw into the pond. As for the fish, the highest bidder could only catch less than one hundred kilos. Both the bidders lost money.

Look out for data. Don't speculate and go with the voice of the crowd.

25. THE IMAGE

You are a success and in your lifetime: 1) created large enterprises, 2) a powerful politician, 3) well known in the arts, 4) a decorated soldier, or 5) world renowned scientist. When you die, what image/photograph is going to be associated with your biography?

Most often the picture taken when the person was in the ages 30-50 will be associated with his/her biography.

The ages 30-50 are the most productive years of one's life. Of course, there are people whose productive years span beyond 80, but they are rare.

People only remember your work and its impact on the society. They will not remember your wealth, spouse, children or family, unless they are also well-known.

Work hard, work smart, make an impact.

26. MAN'S LIFE

Man lives to please his tongue, eyes and head. First love is his tongue. He feeds gourmet foods to please his tongue. He goes the extra mile to take care of the tongue. In fact he is living to please his tongue. The tongue helps him make a living.

Next priority is his eyes. Every man would like to see everything - good, racy and bad. Even if he is warned not to see something, he sees it on the sly.

Man pleases his head by indulging in spirits. He indulges in spirits so as to be out of reality, albeit for a short period of time.

27. THE APPLE TREE

Farmer Nick had a large apple orchard. Nick's orchard was famous for his juicy apples. Every year while collecting his apples, farmer Nick would grade his apples.

The good looking large apples were collected and packed carefully. They headed to high-end grocery stores. The second grade apples were collected in plastic bags and they headed to ordinary grocery stores. The not-so-desirable apples were turned to apple sauce; some of them were made into apple cider. The half rotten ones were provided to the animals in the farm or converted to manure. None of the apples in Nick's farm was wasted.

Once students graduate from a college, not every one turns to be movie stars, CEO's or political leaders who are visible in the society. Every one takes a job or will have a job that is useful to the society. Unlike a fruit, man is resilient, he can transform into any roll if he puts in some effort. A man who is a clerk today can become a CEO tomorrow due to his hard work and persistence. Similarly, a waiter can become a movie star; a cleaner can become a head cook if he or she desires.

Everyone is valuable and unique. You are here for a reason; discover who you are.

28. THE CRASH

One summer Ben was invited by his friends for a meeting at a restaurant. Since it was fine weather, they decided to dine outside.

There were cheap plastic tables and chairs outside the restaurant for clients interested to dine out. Ben and his friends talked about their work and the "good old days."

The waiter arrived after some time; Ben and his friends ordered food. The food arrived in ten minutes.

When Ben ate food, he felt uneasiness. The chair seemed to behave awkward. Whenever Ben placed food in his mouth, the chair's legs moved.

When Ben ate food, his weight increased. After some time the chair could no longer tolerate Ben's weight; finally the chair split into two. Luckily, Ben caught on the table that prevented his fall. There must have been a small crack on the chair before Ben arrived that increased with time, splitting the chair.

Man is born free; he is also given free will to choose whatever he wants. Whatever one does, karma follows him.

It is not prudent to build empires on the blood and tears of others. You could be the king of your empire only for a limited time. When your bad karma outweighs your luck, your fortune topples.

Everything is received in packages; luck is received in packages, so is tragedy. When you build a house of ill-gotten wealth or wealth made abusing others, often it comes crashing like a house of cards after sometime.

You cannot call a man lucky at any point in his life. We can assess if a man was lucky only after he has passed away.

29. WINDOW OF OPPORTUNITY

Ben and Collin were from an upper middle-class family on either side of the city. They never crossed path during the student years. Ben was a hard worker. He studied quickly. His parents gave him assignments and he learned his parent's business. He was also good in art. His uncle recommended him to an artist, who taught him painting. Ben liked his art teacher's paintings and recommended his father to commission 25 paintings.

Ben had to take care of the family business after his father's early demise when he was just 27 years of age. Luckily, Ben had completed a master's degree in business administration and worked for few years at a large company. Ben jumped into any opportunity that was offered to him. Since Ben learned everything before his father's death, he could easily run his father's enterprise. Ben's art teacher became famous and suddenly the paintings that Ben's father commissioned commanded a royal price. Ben's agriculture land was now close to the developing city and the land price multiplied many folds. Ben used his talents to build homes and offices in his land.

On the other side of town, Collin was wasting his time on expensive cars and vacations. He did not grow any of his talents. Collin was offered internship in many of his father's friend's companies, which he rejected. Collin's father lost his business during a recession, and he was unable to work due to a stroke. Collin had no talents and could not independently run any business. Collin had to take care of his family. He applied for a job and got a position as a clerk in the Ben's office. He struggled hard to run his family.

Opportunities doesn't last forever. There is no guarantee that your parents and siblings are around way into your adulthood. It is better to learn everything quickly. There is also no guarantee that there will be good teachers and friends that will motivate you and recommend you in your life. Any talents you grow at a young age will benefit later.

30. THE WORLD DOES NOT WAIT FOR ANYONE

A mama goose built a nest on the roof of the portico of the Institute. A couple of days later she laid 5 eggs. Weeks later, the eggs hatched and 5 beautiful goslings emerged. Three days later it was time for the mama to feed the goslings.

The mama goose jumped from the roof of the portico. After a little bit of hesitation, the first gosling jumped from the roof and followed his mama. Three goslings followed the first gosling. The mama goose and the four goslings waited for the fifth gosling to jump. However, the fifth gosling was crying and walking helter-skelter on the roof. The mama goose called out her baby for several minutes. She was anxious; she had to feed her babies and find a place to rest.

After half-an-hour of crying and yelling, the mama goose and four goslings walked away to a nearby stream. The fifth gosling was afraid and still crying and walking on the roof without following her family.

Unknown to the mama goose, high above the Institute was a hawk seeing the drama below. When the mama goose and the four goslings left, the hawk had lunch.

The world does not wait for anyone.

31. GOAL

Football (soccer) is the most popular sport of the planet. Even, if people have not played it, they must have watched someone play it. Football is a team sport. Every individual has to play their part effectively. The ball does not travel unopposed at any time during the game. The stronger the opposing team, less the number of goals. There is a huge applause when a team strikes a goal.

Everyone has goal(s) in their life. In fact, life is accomplishment of a series of goals. It is not easy to strike a goal. There may be many people who oppose it along the way. Keep on playing. You will accomplish your goals sooner than you think.

32. CORNERED AT THE CORNER

Ken and Kevin were classmates and were also neighbors. Ken was from a lower-middle class family, whereas Kevin was from an upper-middle class family. Kevin was smart and bright in his studies. Ken was an average student; however, he was active in several non-profit organizations. He had good leadership skills that he used to successfully run several programs for the non-profits. Ken's father struggled to educate Ken.

One day Kevin was asked by his teacher to help Ken in Math and Science that he was not doing well. Kevin ignored his teacher's plea. Kevin did not want Ken to score good grades. Kevin was always the top in his class, and he wanted to maintain the status quo.

After school, Kevin made it through the best University in the country. Ken ended up at a community college. Ken studied Finance and Accountancy.

Kevin's university encouraged team work. Kevin's team member, Timothy was really helpful. Timothy forwarded all the study notes to Kevin, whereas Kevin hid all the study materials.

At the tail end of the final semester, Kevin was approached by a bank for a job. During the interview, Kevin was asked by the hiring manager whether he would recommend some of his classmates for more jobs at the bank. Kevin bluffed, "I think every student in my class is hired by companies."

Kevin was elated that he got a good position at a big bank. Kevin was placed in the mortgage division of the bank. His office was in a corner of the building, facing the wall of a neighboring building!

Unknown to Kevin was that someone was following him for a long time - Karma. Of the major divisions in the bank, the mortgage division was the under performer. No matter how hard Kevin worked, the division didn't do well. Kevin tried to move out; none of the companies were interested in Kevin as his division was not doing well and the figures were in the public domain.

Kevin's former classmate and neighbor Ken performed really well in College. He worked also as a teaching aid and was compensated for the job. Ken's students performed well in their studies. Ken's professor recommended him to an alumni at a large IT company, when he requested a smart student for his firm.

Ken did exceptionally well in his company; he also enrolled in the continuing education program of the company and took an E-MBA in

Finance and Management from a prestigious university. Eventually, Ken became the CEO of the organization; he managed the company really well and made it to the top of the Fortune 500 list.

Whether talented or not talented; with social skills or without social skills; compassionate or not compassionate; karma follows you.

33. ORGANIZATION AS A TREE

Every organization (or country) can be compared to a fruit tree. You are enjoying the fruits of an organization (or country) set up by someone's hard work. Now it is your responsibility to nurture and grow the tree so that the next generation can enjoy its fruits. Eating a trees fruit without caring for it, watering or fertilizing will ultimately impact the productivity of the tree. Work hard, keep up with the latest information, innovate, and make yourself proud that you did something for the current and next generation.

34. THE NUTMEG

In the tropics, the nutmeg trees are cultivated for its seed and the surrounding mace. They are a presence in the homestead of the tropics. The seeds are collected from the fruit hanging on the tree or if fallen, from the ground. The family members collect the nutmeg seeds if there are nutmeg trees in the homestead.

As I was busy with work, I recently asked our new hire to collect the nutmeg seeds. She came back with just four seeds. "I could only find these", the new hire remarked.

I knew I could find more seeds if I combed the area myself. The following day, I took a plastic bag and started collecting the nutmeg seeds.

Within a few hours my small plastic bag was full of nutmeg seeds. I weighed them – two kilos.

When you are an employer, keep your eyes wide open. Have an eye on the behavior of your employees.

35. THE SEA WALL

Large granite stones were placed around the port city to protect against sea erosion. The granite stones were covered with algae and sea bird droppings with time. Not far from the sea wall was granite covered elegant buildings. The buildings housed offices of large and famous companies.

The granite stones on the gleamy buildings used to make fun of the granite stones making up the sea wall. Those stones did not utter a word back when provoked; they always kept a low profile.

Years passed. One day a hurricane was heading towards the city. The granite stones of the sea wall said, "The time has arrived to show who we are. Hold tight. Never move an inch. We should stay strong to protect the city".

The hurricane hit the city hard. The buildings facing the sea were afraid that they would be destroyed. The mighty waves lashed at the sea wall. The granite stones of the sea wall did not move. They defended the city. The granite buildings saw how the stones of the sea defended the city.

After a day, the hurricane passed by; the city had no damages. The news was out how the sea wall protected the city. The granite stones of the buildings apologized to the stones on the sea wall for making fun of them; they also thanked them for protecting them.

36. WORK IN PROGRESS

Daniel worked hard for his company. His strategies helped his company be the best in the state. With time, Daniel was promoted as the Vice President of the company. Several years later the management merged the company with a competitor. The new management replaced several executives; Daniel lost his job. Though Daniel wanted to start his own business, his wife, Mrs. Claire did not encourage him. "You have worked your entire life, you should now take some rest," said Mrs. Claire. Daniel also had second thoughts; ultimately, Daniel retired from work and stayed home.

Daniel's son, Steve did not like his father retiring. He knew that if his father would have started a business it would have been very successful. Alas, he did not have any voice!

Years later, Steve also joined a company. He worked very hard. Steve made sure the company made good profit every year. During a recession cycle, the company did not make huge profits as anticipated. The company laid off a percentage of their workforce. Steve's job was also on the chopping block. Steve went home and thought what he could do. He had good technical and management skills. He remembered years earlier when his father retired after the lay-off. He did not wish to follow his father's example. Steve knew that laying off may be a blessing in disguise.

Steve immediately set up a company. He talked to his former clients if they could provide some business. Steve's quotations were lower than other competitors. Within a week Steve got enough clients that he employed a couple of people at his new company. With time, Steve's company grew into a Fortune 500 company.

Our career is a work in progress. Lay off and termination from a company is part of life and is a phase in our career. In fact, lay off has always advanced career for people willing to try again. Your good karma at the previous organization is waiting to pay back; hence, never give up.

37. COFFEE TIME

The church provided coffee and cookies after the Sunday service. The parishioners lined up to get coffee and cookies so as to socialize after the Sunday service. The coffee ran out after some time. People at the end of the line were disappointed as they could not get coffee when they opened the coffee urn faucet.

Larry, who was standing in the line, watched what others were doing. When he came in front of the coffee urn he tilted the coffee urn and opened the faucet. He filled his coffee cup. The people behind Larry cheered, "That was smart."

Think different.

38. THE DRIVER

Paul was the founder and CEO of a large company. However hard he tried, his company couldn't overtake the largest company in the domain. Paul wanted to diversify his company, but the shareholders and investors had mandated that Paul could do whatever he wished, only if his company would be No. 1 in the domain.

Once Paul was driving through the suburbs; at one point his was the lead vehicle. After few minutes, when Paul reached a traffic light, there was an old vehicle before him. Since it was a one lane road, Paul had to follow him. Paul felt frustrated as his vehicle was forced to go slow. After sometime Paul noticed that whenever the driver in front fell on a sunken manhole, Paul could maneuver it. At that instance Paul had an idea.

Paul went home and read about the competing company and its business tactics. He understood the mistakes and blunders in business committed by the competing company. In a couple of years Paul's company became the number one company of the domain.

39. THE CARROT

I decided to grow carrots in our backyard. Carrots grow best in loose soil rich in organic matter. The soil in our backyard is clayey. I did not know how the carrots would turn up during harvest. I planted as many carrot seedlings in the vegetable garden; the rest I planted in several pots containing loose soil. I manured the carrots in the garden as well as the pots and they looked lush and green in a couple of weeks. After four months it was time to harvest carrots. I pulled the carrot plants in the vegetable garden. Alas, the carrots were small and twisted. The clayey structure prevented the carrot from penetrating into the soil. The deformed carrots and its leaves landed in the cage of children's pet rabbit, "Puffy."

Later, I pulled the carrot from the pots. The carrots were straight and long as in a grocery store. The loose soil in the pot induced the carrots to form straight roots.

When you work for reputed companies, people in your inner circle think that you are a lucky person. Just working in a reputed company does not automatically qualify you as a great employee. You have to take the initiative to start innovative projects. If the atmosphere in the reputed company is not conducive, you will have "dull projects" that do not help your career. During a recession or lay-off while hunting for a job, your CV will have few accomplishments to entice the hiring managers.

40. THE ROCKET

Once a new aerospace company launched a rocket with a sophisticated communication satellite. The company tested and re-tested all the parts before the launch. The satellite was supposed to last for at least thirty years. Hundreds of scientists and technicians worked round-the-clock to realizing their dream.

The rocket had a picture-perfect launch. Unfortunately, the satellite did not work as anticipated. The solar antennas never unfolded, and the electronics did not receive the commands from the earth station. Several weeks later the mission was aborted; the satellite was eventually destroyed by a meteor.

Most parents prepare the children to succeed in school and college. It is the duty of the children to work hard and achieve good grades and pursue higher studies. Parents can only push their kids to a particular limit or provide a strong foundation; the children have to build over it.

Similarly, an employer can only give limited guidance to a new hire (employee). The employee must eventually give new ideas to the employer. The employer also must be receptive to new ideas and slowly transform the organization.

The current global literacy rate is around 90 percent. In another decade, it will be complete literacy. The twenty-first century is the age of information, one cannot survive without education. Currently, most people have access to a smart phone. The smart phones and computers helped students during the COVID pandemic as teaching was over the phone and computer. One can learn any skill over the phone. In fact, a phone is a must as several services are provided by government and other organizations over the phone.

Technology and business are rapidly changing. The employees have to read and understand new trends and also update their skills to move their company forward. The employer's and supervisor's guidance are not just enough to grow a company; most information is redundant within a few months. Hence, every employee has to come up with new ideas to grow the company.

The competition is no longer local, but rather global. A company can have new technologies and skillful people from any corner of the planet. Most jobs are getting automated. People should educate and re-educate to stay relevant.

41. THE SUN WILL EMERGE FROM THE CLOUD

You cannot hide a talented person forever; he will emerge at the right time. Years back Mike was an engineer at a photographic film company. Mike was responsible for developing new and innovative films for the company.

Mike read the latest science and technology journals. One day he came up with the idea of filmless camera. Mike showed his supervisor Pablo his new device. Though Pablo liked the concept, he did not want to jeopardize his companies existing products; he also didn't wish to see Mike elevated to a senior position due to his discovery. Hence, Palo dumped Mike's idea and asked him to concentrate only on films.

Mike understood the importance of his discovery. He slowly reached out to electronics companies for a job. One of the companies was interested in Mike's ideas.

During the interview the President of the company inquired how long does he need to make a product using the new technology. Mike answered, "One year."

Within one year Mike developed the prototype and eventually the company started selling filmless digital cameras. Mike was later promoted to the Senior Vice President within a year and later became the President of the company.

42. FREE LUNCH

Gustav invited his friends for lunch during the weekend. The friends brought snacks, desserts and other eatables. After lunch, Gustav requested his friends to help him move the sofa and other furniture to the basement as he was expecting new furniture the following week.

Months later, Gustav again invited his friends for lunch. Once the friends enjoyed the meal, Gustav took them to the garage. He pointed to a new generator and requested, "Could you help me move it to the side of the house."

"Of course," his friends replied.

Gustav's friends understood that he was not genuine. He was offering his friends free meal in the pretext of making them do odd jobs. They would have eagerly helped him if requested.

Later, when Gustav invited his friends for lunch or dinner no one showed up!

43. EPICENTER OF LEARNING

At the start of the nineteenth century the kingdoms of the Indian subcontinent were in disarray. The rigid social structure prevented progress to multitude of the population. Industrialization had not yet started in the Indian subcontinent. Industrialization requires literacy. The literacy rate in India was around 10 percent.

The London Missionary Society headed by William Tobias Ringeltaube started a school in the southern tip of the kingdom of Travancore in the beginning years of the nineteenth century. Years later, the school had an important guest from the capital city: Maharaja Swathi Thirunal Rama Varma, the King of Travancore.

The young King liked the school and its curriculum. He wished to have a similar school in Trivandrum, the capital city. The King asked the headmaster if he could take the lead if a similar school was setup in Trivandrum, to which the headmaster agreed. The Raja's Free School eventually metamorphosed to the Maharaja's University College that trained leaders (people with a purpose) in several walks of life.

The future rulers of Travancore replicated similar schools all over the kingdom. The kingdom spent a good part of its revenue for education and healthcare. By 1950, the Kingdom of Travancore had a literacy rate of fifty percent.

Many kingdoms and non-profit organizations of the Indian subcontinent created epicenters of learning before independence. The literacy rate improved with time.

After independence, every state of India gave priority to education. The schools started free meal schemes to encourage children to study. Eventually the whole country progressed. Industrialization paved way to Information Technology and other service industries. The good quality technical and management education led to the rise of super technologists and managers now leading large corporate houses all over the world.

The seed you plant today will nourish the future population.

44. LAYERS

When paleontologists dig for fossils they observe different strata each containing organisms from a different age. Similarly, when archeologists excavate specimens from regions that had been home to people for several millennia they see each layer of soil occupied by different civilizations or kingdoms.

Though we are currently on the surface of earth, with time we will also be part of a geological layer. We will be known for what we did or did not do.

45. THE COLLEGE KID

Bruce graduated from high school. He wished to take a biology degree and upon completion go for a medical degree. Bruce applied to all the nearby Universities. Bruce enrolled at a university that was only three-hour drive from home.

Bruce's parents and relatives warned about the university resident life. They asked Bruce to only be friends with like-minded students. As he wished to be a physician, Bruce's parents asked him to work in college laboratories after class so that he could get authorship in journal papers that would impact his medical school admission.

Once Bruce reached the university, he changed his behavior. He joined all the clubs, partied hard, never went to a laboratory in the evening hours; he enjoyed the "ultimate freedom."

Bruce's grades plummeted. His parents received warnings from the university. Finally, the parents removed Bruce from the university. They asked him to enter the family business.

Man has a choice; he can choose either good or evil. If he forgoes the good values; the bad ones take its place. Children that do not listen to the good advice of their parents or other elders have a tendency to listen to people that introduce bad behaviors.

There is no age a man can turn to evil deeds. In some trades, the peers offer new recruits tobacco or alcohol. Some people think that "to go with the flow" they have to use tobacco or alcohol so as to impress their peers and get into their "good books."

Not everyone has the "will power" to quit smoking or quit spirits later in life. Many people cannot quit smoking or drinking once they start the bad habit; that may ultimately impact their health leading to death.

Learn to say NO. You should control your life, not others. You are responsible for your life as well as others associated with you.

46. VERY IMPORTANT PERSON

Johann and Jaiden were brothers. One day they received a gift by mail from a relative. The children opened the gift and found two cars, one was a radio controlled vehicle and the other non-automatic vehicle.

The brothers began to fight for the automatic car. One stated that he is the elder and is the important member of the family; the other stated that he is the youngest member of the family and is the darling of "pop and mom".

The dad heard the quarrel and took the children to their room. He asked the children to complete a jigsaw puzzle that was in a box in the corner of their room.

Once completed, the dad asked the elder son to take out the least favored piece (tab) on the jigsaw puzzle. The elder son removed a tab from the jigsaw puzzle.

The dad asked the younger son, "What do you think of the jigsaw puzzle with a missing piece?"

The young son replied, "There is a hole in the jigsaw puzzle. I think every piece is important."

Every man is important and is here for a purpose. Absence of someone creates a hole in the life of people associated with that person.

47. THE WOOD

There was once a large white oak tree in a forest. Only the forest officials knew of its existence since it was deep in the forest. The oak was a very large tree that six grown adults could wrap their arms around the tree trunk. The white oak tree was very old; many birds made the tree their home. There were plenty of lichens, moss and other fungi growing on the oak tree. In addition, there were innumerable insects living on its bark. The oak tree generated tonnes of oxygen every year.

Adjacent to the white oak tree was a walnut tree. The white oak and the walnut trees would always communicate. The white oak tree would lament that its growth benefited only a few organisms of the forest. The walnut tree would encourage and motivate the oak tree. The walnut said to the Oak, "Half the birds in the forest are living on your branches."

Years passed, one dark night there was a stormy rain. Sometime during the midnight the walnut heard a ground shaking loud noise. The walnut did not understand what was happening around. Early morning the walnut saw the oak lying uprooted.

Many hours later the forest officials toured the area and saw the fallen majestic white oak tree. They measured the tree. It was the largest specimen in the country. The forest officials quickly arranged an auction. The famous lumber company Harry and Sons won the auction.

Harry and Sons had recently received bids to furnish several important offices. They used the wood of white oak tree to build a new desk and chair for the President of the country.

In addition, the wood of the white oak tree was used to make lectern for several university departments, altar for a cathedral, book racks for the city public library, and furniture for the children's hospital. The small pieces of the wood were used to make specialized pens.

The majestic white oak tree provided shelter to many organisms in its life time; it also was useful after its death.

48. INFLUENCE

Martin was driving with his elderly cousin Thompson on a three lane highway. They were heading to a family event. Martin was driving on the right lane. In front of Martin was a van, after some time the van moved to the middle lane. Martin was still on the right lane. The maximum speed was 65 miles per hour. Martin maintained the legal speed. A couple of minutes later there was a truck in front of Martin.

Martin followed the truck in front of him; his speed decelerated to 60 miles per hour. The neighboring lanes were empty. After some time, Cousin Thompson stated, "Martin your speed is influenced by the vehicle in front of you. If you follow the vehicle in front of you, your speed is influenced by their speed, naturally you will drive slowly and we will be late for the family function."

The words of cousin Thompson was an eye opener for Martin. He changed his driving tactics.

Martin was an entrepreneur; he always used to follow the tactics and strategies of his competitors. His products lacked innovation; all his products were "me too products" and had poor response in the market.

Martin understood his drawbacks; he wrote a plan in his diary. He set up a small research and development (R and D) department and employed creative scientists and technicians. The R and D department developed innovative products that were a big success among the masses. Martin licensed his products to large companies all over the world.

49. EXERCISE

The hands of the clock are a family. The second hand is the fastest, it is fit and thin. The minute hand is slower; however, it is also slim. The short hour hand moves very slowly, you can barely see it move; maybe that is why it is obese.

50. JOSEPH THE GOVERNOR

One of the motivating characters of the Bible is Joseph, the son of Jacob, who became the Governor of Egypt.

Changing gear; in Mahabharata, there is a story of the prince Abhimanyu entering the padmavyuham (a military formation) for the battle. He was successful in entering padmavyuham for the battle; however, he was not trained to exit; and that proved fatal.

Everybody wishes to be a leader of a company, organization or country. Every leader enters those entities with much fanfare. However, most often, they fail running those entities.

Now coming back to the character Joseph the Governor; he was one of the most successful governors in the Bible. His policies prevented hunger and starvation, not only for the people of Egypt, but also for the people of the neighboring countries.

How did Joseph become successful as a Governor. Going through his history, we read that as a boy, he was in charge of some of Jacob's sheep and cattle. The Bible says that he multiplied the sheep and cattle; whereas his brother's fared poorly. Meaning, he knew animal husbandry.

After, Joseph was sold into slavery, Potiphar recognized his talents and made him charge of his estate. Joseph multiplied the harvest and filled the barns. Meaning, Joseph knew agriculture.

When Joseph was thrown into the prison, the prison officials understood Joseph's abilities and made him charge of running the prison. Meaning, Joseph knew how to handle criminals and thugs.

When Joseph was made the Governor of Egypt by the Pharaoh, his immediate goal was to improve animal husbandry (the fertilizer in those days was animal dung and the cattle were also the tractors of that age), increase farm produce and build barns for storing grains. Joseph was trained in every aspects. Since Joseph had experience handling criminals, he didn't have to be taught how to handle contractors and government officials.

Joseph's training and experience in his life made him a successful governor. Sometimes life may take you through difficult circumstances. Remember, those are just lessons for a big purpose.

51. THE FIRST CHRISTMAS

The young and old of the world look forward to celebrate Christmas. Christmas signals the end of the year. Children are happy that the year-end exams are over and look forward to receiving gifts from parents, relatives and friends. The workers would think about the productivity and companies would ponder about the revenue generated during the year.

Though the festival is a joyous occasion, the first Christmas was not a joyful event, at least initially for a young family. The family knocked on the door of houses and every inn to find a place for their baby to be born. The couple could not find a room until someone at an inn pointed to a nearby stable. Any family would be sad to have their baby born in a manger.

Sometimes in life we are pushed to conditions or places that we do not like to be in, due to the ridicule or stigma we would likely face. Often times, the bad phases in life are temporary, one would move to a better phase after some time. Tough times don't last, tough people do, After the baby was born in the manger, the shepherds were the first visitors. They recommended a house for the new family. It was in that house the three wise men visited the baby months later. We do not know the house where the baby was raised for a few months, but the stable on a hillock where the baby was born was transformed to the Church of Nativity.

It is said that the stable had a lone ox. Until that moment in history ox, goat and sheep were offered by mankind to please the divine. (It is impossible for the blood of bulls and goats to take away sins. - Hebrews 10:4). Here you have a scene where the offering (ox) is facing the offeree. Animals ceased to be offered as an offering when the offeree became the offering years later on a cross.